LET'S TALK SEX AND STDS

THE STUDENT EDITION

DR. KATINA DAVIS-KENNEDY, EdD, MSN, ARNP, FNP-C

Copyright © 2017 Dr. Katina Davis-Kennedy

All rights reserved. No part of this publication may be reproduced, distributed, or transmitted in any form or by any means, this includes: photocopying, recording, or other electronic or mechanical methods, without the prior written permission of the publisher, except in the case of brief quotations embodied in critical reviews and certain other noncommercial uses permitted by copyright law.

ISBN-10: 1-945532-48-3
ISBN-13: 978-1-945532-48-1

Printed in the United States of America

For permission requests, write to the publisher, addressed "Attention: Permissions Coordinator," at the address below.

info@opportunepublishing.com
www.opportunepublishing.com

Disclaimer
Although the author and publisher have made every effort to ensure that the information in this book was correct at press time, the author and publisher do not assume and hereby disclaim any liability to any party for any loss, damage, or disruption caused by errors or omissions, whether such errors or omissions result from negligence, accident, or any other cause.

Call to Press

If you are interested in booking this author for readings or other events, please use the contact information below:

Email: Katinadkennedy@gmail.com

Website: www.drkatinakennedy.com

Facebook: DrKatinaKennedy

Instagram: @Katinakennedynursepractitioner

YouTube: NurseK Kennedy

About the Author

Dr. Katina Davis-Kennedy resides in sunny Ft. Lauderdale, Florida. She has been in the nursing profession since 2003 and has continued to build such an adept career within the medical industry. Dr. Davis-Kennedy began her journey studying nursing at Florida A&M University, and then went on to complete her master's in nursing at Florida Atlantic University and doctoral degree in educational leadership at the University of Phoenix.

Dr. Davis-Kennedy was a Registered Nurse (RN) for four years in the medical surgical trauma and critical care unit. She is currently a certified Family Nurse Practitioner (FNP) that practices primary care medicine, teen and women's health. In order to feed her unfilled appetite for promoting health and wellness, she spends her extra time getting others to be physically active and maintain a healthy lifestyle.

She is an advocate for getting and staying physically fit in order to manage and treat chronic diseases such as high blood pressure, high cholesterol, diabetes, and much more. In her community, she instructs multiple exercise classes and camps in order to build awareness and encourage a healthier lifestyle.

Not only is Dr. Davis-Kennedy a nursing professor, Family Nurse Practitioner, health educator and fitness motivator, but she also shows her passion for health by being a healthy-living motivational speaker and author.

"I aspire to inspire others to transform into their higher capabilities."

–Dr. Katina Davis-Kennedy

Acknowledgments

I want to thank my family and friends for standing behind me and never allowing me to give up on my dreams; especially my mom, mother-in-law, dad, sisters and son. To my very supportive husband, Stephen Kennedy, you have been my rock, my love, and my world.

In addition, I would like to give a personal thanks to my older sister Trenesa Davis for her unwavering support and countless hours of help on this project.

A special thanks to my colleague Shalonna Battle for her expertise and contribution, as well as to my publisher, Shanley at Opportune Publishing, for exceptional hard work and dedication to helping me put my idea in stone. To my nephew, Aaron Davis with A Davis Illustration, thank you for designing the book cover.

Last, but not least, I would like to thank you for purchasing this book and allowing yourself to become educated on an important topic. You rock!!

Table of contents

Preface 13
Chapter 1: Know Your Body 17
Chapter 2: What is a Sexually Transmitted Disease? 25
Chapter 3: All about STDs 27

Chapter 4: Bacterial Sexually Transmitted Diseases 29

Chapter 5: Viral Sexually Transmitted Diseases 37
        Hepatitis B 37
        Hepatitis C 39
        Genital Herpes 40
        HIV/AIDS 42
        Human Papillomavirus (HPV) 45

Chapter 6: Other STDs 49

        Trichomoniasis (Trich) 49
        Chancroid 51
        Lymphogranuloma Venereum (LGV) 52
        Pediculosis Pubis 53
        Scabies 54
        Molluscum 56

Chapter 7: Student Do's and Don'ts 59

Chapter 8: Advice for the Student 63

Chapter 9: Wrap Up 67

Glossary 71

Preface

Do you believe you have enough knowledge to take the next step, or get past third base? For those of you who do not, here is a helping hand to get you ready. Education is important before embarking on a major responsibility such as *sex*. In this book, you will find all the information you will need in order to step into the world of sex.

I have created this guide for students and others who are seeking to become more knowledgeable about sex, physical body changes, and STDs. There are a lot of rumors and misleading information being spread around. Therefore, it's very important that you are not one of those people being miseducated. Sometimes it can be the difference between life and death. It is important that before you engage in sexual activities, you are aware of the male and female genitalia (genitalia pictures can be found at the end of this chapter) and various STDs that can affect the human body. Doing this can help to answer any questions you may have.

When is it a good time to talk to your parents about sex?

This is one of the most controversial questions floating around. It may be weird, embarrassing, or scary. However, anytime you have questions about sex or sexual activities, please talk to your parents. There is a lot of wrong information floating around with friends and the internet, but your parents can help with clarifying those myths. Remember, your friends have just about the same amount of knowledge that you have, so you want to talk to someone who is older and has your best interest at heart.

The introduction to sex goes by many different names: the birds and the bees, the delivery stork and the infamous "Talk." Psychologists believe "The Talk" can start as early as nine years of age, but definitely should be discussed in the pre-teens (nine to 12 years old).

It can be difficult to openly talk about sex because the expectation is to wait until you're married or are old enough, however old that is to your parents.

Realistically and unfortunately, sexual activity may occur as early as nine years old. Once you are nearing or enter middle school, you have likely been exposed to many different sexual advances from others that are usually more experienced and have more information, no matter if it's right or wrong.

Every so often patterns change amongst youth. For example, when your parents were your age, they didn't do certain sexual things that younger people are doing now. But, either way, nothing new has been invented, so your parents can relate to whatever acts, rumors or things that are new to you. Make sure you are using your parents as your primary resource for information about sex.

There has been a huge epidemic that has recently come

to light: oral sex practices are vastly prevalent in the middle school population. You may have giggled at the sight of that information, but it's a very serious thing. Without being properly prepared, you could become a victim of an STD or an unwanted pregnancy before you have had the opportunity to gain accurate sexual knowledge. Middle schoolers range in age from 11 to 14 years old. Imagine an 11-year-old being pregnant. As crazy as it sounds, that's a very realistic vision that can come to life when middle school students are having oral sex and experimenting with other sexual behaviors.

Ideally, you want to beat those outside influences to the punch. *Let's Talk Sex & STDs: The Student Edition* is here to help you become more knowledgeable. It's not to threaten you or to make you feel bad about sex; it's to educate you on doing things the right way, and making sure you are being safe 100% of the time.

This book isn't bolstering you to go have sex; it's a great idea for everyone to wait till they are of age and/or married. But if you do act and don't wait, it is important that you are knowledgeable about the possible consequences of having sex.

Chapter 1: Know Your Body

Puberty

Puberty is when the body grows and develops causing changes in the physical appearance. We all must go through it. The stages of puberty can be scary and exciting. However, knowing what to expect during puberty will help you overcome fear and go through it prepared.

There is not a set age of when you will go through puberty. Girls may start puberty between the ages of 8 and 13 and may experience a growth spurt between 10 and 14. Boys develop between the ages of 10 and 13 and grow until they are around 16. Eating healthy, exercising, and getting adequate sleep are important during puberty years and will help with proper growth and development.

Generally, we all know what to expect as we are growing up. We can look at our parents and other adults and notice they have different features than you do. For example, men have facial hair, and most young boys don't. Women have breasts formed, and when girls are young, they don't have much of anything on their chest.

Puberty: Changes in Girls

As a female, your body will start to noticeably change. You will go through things you never did as a child and you will eventually become a woman.

Being on your way to becoming a woman means that:

- You will develop breasts and your hips will become rounded.

- You will have an increase in height.

- Six to 12 months after your breasts began to develop, you will start growing hair on your vagina (public hair) and under your arms.

- The size of your female genitals such as the labia, vagina, clitoris, and uterus will increase.

- You will begin *menstruation*, also known as your period. The average age this happens is about 12 years old, however, it may be dependent upon when your mom first started her period.

- You will reach your adult height around 14 or 15 years of age.

What is a Menstruation/Period?

Menstruation, also known as a monthly period, is when a woman bleeds from her vagina every month. Periods typically last from three to five days, however, it can last as long as seven days. Everyone's body is different, so you wouldn't know how long yours will be until you get it. Before the period occurs every month, the female body goes through a menstrual cycle. Regular menstrual cycles are an indication the body is working normally. However, don't be alarmed; during teen years, the menstrual cycle may be irregular when going through hormonal changes. This means one month you could have your period for three days and the next month it's seven days, if you get it at all that month. The older you get, the more your body will know what it wants to do regularly.

Every person has hormones in their body, which indicate your sex as a person. The lady hormone is called estrogen, and the male hormone is called testosterone.

The menstrual cycle regulates the hormones and prepares the body for pregnancy each month. This sounds extremely scary, but you're not actually going to have a baby. Because you have started puberty you *can* have a baby, and your body prepares itself for that.

The changes in the level of hormones during the month control the menstrual cycle. The cycle is from day one of the period to day one of the next period. On average the menstrual cycle is 28 days long; it can range from 21 to 35 days in adults and 21 to 45 days in teens.

What occurs during the menstrual cycle?

During the first part of the cycle, the level of the estrogen begins to rise. Estrogen is important to a woman's body because it helps build strong bones and is essential for the growth and thickening of the uterus, also known as the womb. The lining of the uterus/womb is where the baby grows if pregnancy occurs.

Additionally, during the rise of estrogen, the lining of the uterus is growing, and an egg or ovum in one of the ovaries starts to grow. Around day 14 of a 28-day cycle, the egg leaves the ovary. This is called ovulation. The egg must go through several areas of your genital system. Check out the diagram below to see where the egg goes while on its journey.

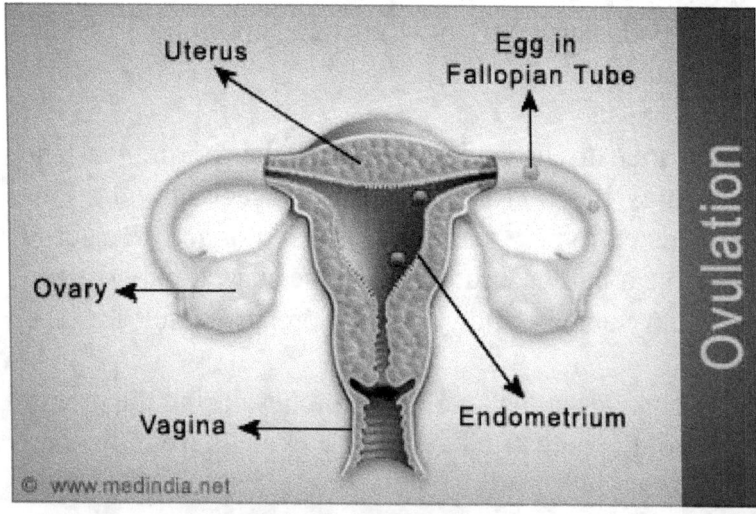

Once the egg leaves the ovary, it goes through the fallopian tube to the uterus. Hormone levels increase to help prepare the uterine lining for pregnancy. Pregnancy occurs if the egg is fertilized by a man's sperm and it attaches to the womb/uterine lining. However, if the egg is not fertilized, it will break apart, the hormone levels will drop, and the period starts.

This process is usually what happens when you have sex with someone without a condom and they ejaculate inside of your vagina. The sperm from a man can only fertilize a female's egg after the male has been or is going through puberty himself.

Puberty: Changes in Boys

When males go through puberty, it's a little different from females. They will experience most of their changes externally. Boys may show initial body changes of puberty between the ages of 10 and 16. Between the ages of 12 and 15 is when they grow the quickest.

Boys' growth spurt occurs about two years later than girls' usually does. By the age of 16, boys stop growing; however, their muscles continue to develop.

When a boy is going through, or has already been through puberty, they will notice these changes: An increase in size of the penis and testicles. Everyone is different, so the increase varies.

- Bodily hair develops on the genitals, which are followed by facial and underarm hair.

- The tone of voice will deepen; "sounding like a man"

- The Adam's apple (in the throat) will get bigger.

- The testicles will begin to produce sperm, which enables them to now fertilize an egg and reproduce with a female.

Male Genitalia

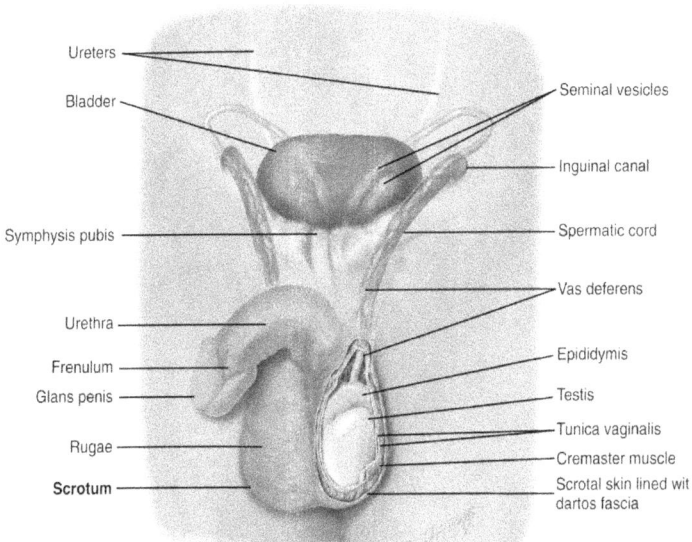

External Female Genitalia

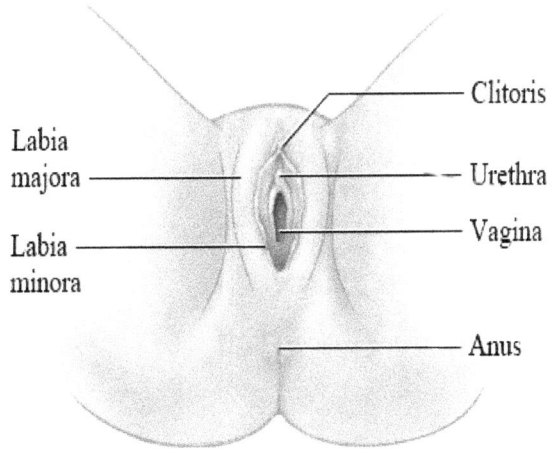

Chapter 2: What is a Sexually Transmitted Disease?

Let's start from the beginning to ensure we are on the same page and all information is consistent and correct.

Sexually Transmitted Diseases (STDs) are diseases that are transmitted or acquired through sexual contact. They are infectious and can spread through:

- Direct skin-to-skin contact.
- Contact with infected bodily fluids.
- Oral, anal, and vaginal sex.
- Saliva, blood, smoking and the use of drugs/needles.

If there is any type of sexual activity, then there is a risk for an STD!

Sexually Transmitted Diseases are called many different things; don't get confused by different terms because they all can be used interchangeably.

Here is a list of some:

- Sexually Transmitted Disease (STD)
- Sexually Transmitted Infection (STI)

- Venereal Disease (VD)

It is important to highlight that STDs are sexually transmitted, which means they can be passed via sexual activities. For example, if a male does not penetrate the vagina, but does rub or touch the area with his penis, this is a sexual activity. If he were infected with an STD, this would be an example of sexually transmitting. Simply touching genitals increase the risk of contracting genital warts, herpes, and other STDs.

This is also true in regard to oral sex. Just Even though there is no insertion of the penis into the vagina, that absolutely does not mean one cannot contract an STD.

This is the importance of educating yourself regarding Sexually Transmitted Diseases. There are many myths and rumors revolving around sex, but misinformation can lead to death.

Chapter 3: All about STDs

Let's Talk Sex & STDs: The Student Edition was created to break down the myths, tell actual facts and disseminate real information in a way that a parent or child would understand. In this chapter, we will go through an array of STDs, some that can be cured and others that cannot.

You will learn about bacterial, viral, and other STDs along with the signs and symptoms to identify if you suspect a STD has been transmitted. It is important that if you recognize any of these symptoms, you seek medical attention immediately. Do not try to cure yourself at home!

Taking the appropriate antibiotics and anti-parasitic medications can cure bacterial and parasitic sexually transmitted infections. However, viral STDs, like HIV/AIDS, are not cured but are managed with anti-viral medications. When it comes to viral STDs, once you've contracted them, you own them!! It is a great time to educate yourself and talk to your parents in order to prevent yourself from obtaining such a life-altering gift.

Chapter 4: Bacterial Sexually Transmitted Diseases

Bacterial sexually transmitted diseases occur when there is a contraction of certain bacterium from another person. This is similar to passing germs to other people and making them sick. These are the STDs that can be cured, luckily.

Chlamydia

Chlamydia is a very common STD, especially among teens. It can be asymptomatic (no symptoms) in females, yet symptomatic in males. If indications are present, they usually show up seven to 28 days after having sex with someone who is infected. However, chlamydia can be detected through tests as early as one to three weeks after contraction, if tested by urine sample or a genital culture (a sample swab of the discharge from the genitals to detect organisms that are bacterial, viral or fungal infections).

There are several ways one can be infected by chlamydia: Through heterosexual and homosexual intercourse; vaginal, anal and oral sex. If you experience any of the symptoms below, you should seek medical attention immediately.

Symptoms amongst females include:
- An abnormal vaginal discharge.
- A burning sensation or pain when urinating.
- Bleeding in between periods.
- Pain during sex.
- Lower abdominal cramping/pain.

Symptoms amongst males include:
- A watery, white discharge from the penis.
- A burning sensation or pain when urinating.
- Frequent urination.
- Pain and swelling in one or both testicles.

Rectal symptoms in both men and women include:
- Discharge
- Rectal pain
- Bleeding

Remember: Chlamydia can be cured with antibiotics. If untreated, this disease can lead to infertility and other very serious complications. A urine sample or genital culture is used to detect chlamydia.

Chlamydia can affect different parts of the body, as shown below.

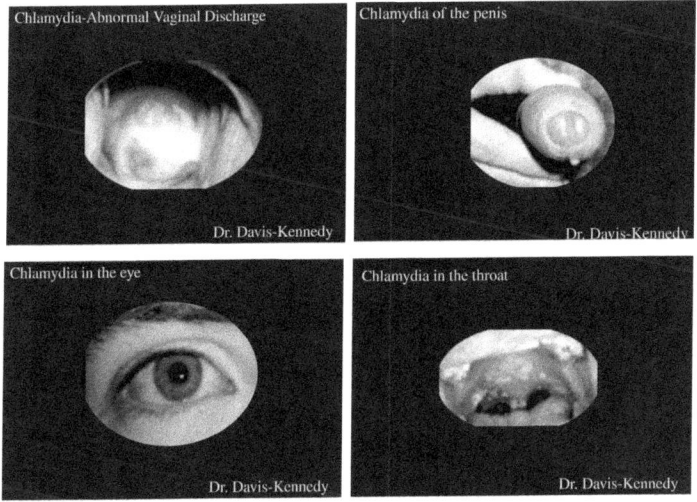

Gonorrhea

Gonorrhea is another common STD, especially among the age group 15-24, according to the Center for Disease Control and Prevention (CDC). Just like chlamydia, it can be present without symptoms, asymptomatic in both males and females, but can be detected at least two to 21 days after being infected. However, it is recommended to wait to be tested two weeks after possible contraction to ensure accurate results.

Gonorrhea ("the clap" or "the drip") is caused by a bacterium called Neisseria Gonorrhea, which can grow and multiply easily within the body. Common areas include: reproductive tract (cervix, uterus, fallopian tubes and urethra), mouth, throat and anus.

This bacterial infection can be contracted vaginally, anally or orally. If you experience any of the symptoms below, you should seek medical attention immediately.

Gonorrhea indicators in men include:

- A burning sensation or pain when urinating.
- A white, yellow, or green discharge from the penis.
- Pain during sex.
- Abnormal frequency of urination.
- Painful or swollen testicles.

Gonorrhea indicators in women include:

- Painful or burning sensation when urinating.
- Green, white or yellow vaginal discharge.
- Lower abdomen pain and cramps.
- Pain during sex.
- Vaginal bleeding between periods.

When a female has gonorrhea symptoms, they are often mild and can be mistaken for a bladder or vaginal infection.

Rectal infections may have indicators in both men and

women that include:

- Discharge
- Anal itching
- Soreness
- Bleeding
- Painful bowel movements

Remember: Gonorrhea can be cured with antibiotics. If untreated, this disease can lead to infertility. A urine sample or genital culture is used to detect gonorrhea. If you experience any of these symptoms, you should seek medical attention immediately.

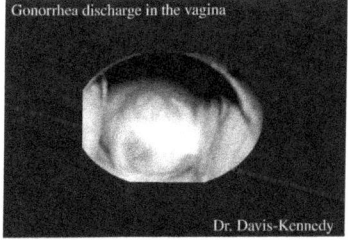
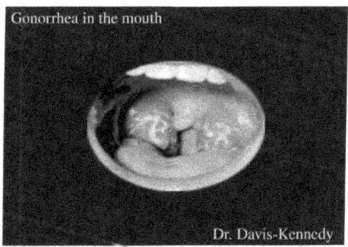
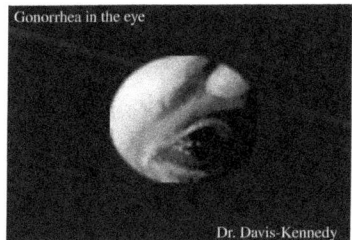
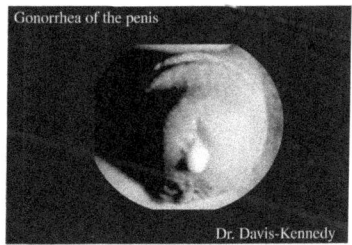

Syphilis

Although *syphilis* is not as prevalent today as it was in the 1960s–1980s, many people are still being infected. This highly contagious disease is spread primarily through sexual activity, including oral and anal sex. Other ways it can be passed on is through prolonged kissing, close bodily contact or open sores. Sores can be found on the penis, vagina, and anus, and sometimes in the rectum, on the lips and in the mouth. Syphilis can also be spread from an infected mother to her unborn baby.

If someone is infected with syphilis, there are several stages they will go through during this infection:

<u>Primary stage:</u> (1-12 weeks after having sex)

- Painless syphilis sore or sores can appear on the mouth or genitals (often confused as an ingrown hair, zipper cut, or harmless bump).

- These sores can last two to six weeks.

*Even after sores aren't present anymore, syphilis is still present.

<u>Second Stage:</u> (new symptoms show up as the sores leave)

- A non-itchy rash appearing on hands, soles of

feet, all over your body or in just a few places.

- You will start experiencing flu-like symptoms: fever, swollen glands, fatigue, muscle aches, headache and sore throat.

- Weight loss occurs.

*Even after rash and flu-like symptoms go away, syphilis is still present.

<u>Latent Stages:</u> (all previous symptoms have gone away)

- Difficulty coordinating muscle movements.
- Paralysis (unable to move certain parts of your body).
- Numbness, blindness, and dementia (mental disorder).
- Damage to internal organs, which can result in death.

If you experience any of the above symptoms, you should seek medical attention immediately.

Remember: Syphilis can be diagnosed through a blood test. Syphilis is a bacterial infection and can be cured with specific antibiotics. However, treatment will not undo any damage caused by the infection. If you experience any of the symptoms, you should seek medical attention immediately; treatment is time sensitive.

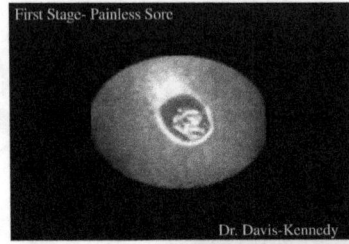
First Stage- Painless Sore

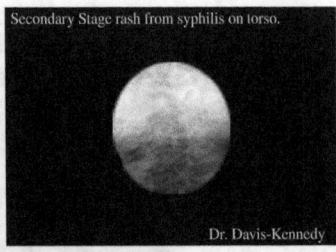
Secondary Stage rash from syphilis on torso.

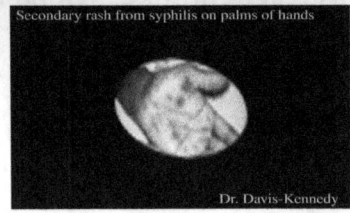
Secondary rash from syphilis on palms of hands

Chapter 5: Viral Sexually Transmitted Diseases

Viruses passed from person-to-person during sexual activity cause viral STDs. In general these infections involve multiple parts of the body simultaneously. There are several infections in this category, including Genital Herpes, HIV/AIDS, Hepatitis B, Hepatitis C and HPV. These are the most serious of all infections to get; they cannot be cured, but there are many treatments that alleviate symptoms.

Hepatitis B

The word hepatitis means "inflammation of the liver". *Hepatitis B* is a virus that can cause scarring of the liver, liver failure, and liver diseases such as cirrhosis and liver cancer.

Hepatitis B is usually transmitted through sex, but can be caused by other things as well, including toxins, certain drugs, some diseases, heavy alcohol use, and bacterial and viral infections. In the U.S., among adults, Hepatitis B is usually spread through sexual contact; this accounts for nearly two-thirds of acute Hepatitis B cases.

Believe it or not, Hepatitis B can be up to 100 times more infectious than HIV. It can be contracted through oral sex with an infected person, male or female.

Hepatitis B can also be spread by:
- Coming in contact with infected blood.
- Sharing needles, razors or toothbrushes with an infected person.
- Childbirth from an infected mother to her baby.

Symptoms for Hepatitis B show up one to nine months after transmission from someone who has Hepatitis B, and are mild or nonexistent.

Women and men with symptoms may notice the following:
- Flu-like symptoms that don't go away
- Fatigue
- Jaundice (yellow skin)
- Joint Pain
- Fever
- Loss of appetite
- Nausea
- Vomiting
- Dark urine
- Light-colored bowel movements.

Remember: Hepatitis B is a viral infection and there is no cure for it. However, there is a vaccine available to protect you from contracting this virus. If you feel you may have come in contact with someone with this infection, a simple blood test is used to detect this virus for diagnosis. If left untreated for a time, it can result in needing a liver transplant, or death.

Hepatitis C

Hepatitis C is very similar to Hepatitis B; you can be infected the same ways:

- From toxins, certain drugs, some diseases and heavy alcohol use.
- Bacterial and viral infections; infected blood; sharing needles, razors and toothbrushes.
- Sexual transmission and childbirth.

In addition, Hepatitis C can be transmitted in other ways, such as getting a tattoo.

Many people have no symptoms or mild symptoms. Symptoms usually appear six to seven weeks after exposure to Hepatitis C. However, this can range from two weeks to six months in certain cases.

Women and men with symptoms may notice the following:

- Flu-like symptoms that don't go away

- Fatigue
- Jaundice (yellow skin)
- Joint Pain
- Fever
- Loss of appetite
- Nausea
- Vomiting
- Dark urine
- Light-colored bowel movements.

Remember: There is no cure for the Hepatitis C virus. However, medications are used to manage this disease. But no cure has been found just yet. If you suspect you may have Hepatitis C, seek medical attention immediately to get a blood test for possible diagnosis. If left untreated, it can result in needing a liver transplant, or death.

Genital Herpes

Genital herpes is a very common sexually transmitted disease caused by the contraction of two viruses: Herpes simplex type 1 and Herpes simplex type 2.

In the United States, about one out of every six people aged 14 to 49 years have genital herpes. You can get herpes by having vaginal, anal or oral sex, as well as genital-to-genital contact with someone who has this viral disease.

The virus is actually carried in the fluid found within the herpes sores; contact with this fluid will cause infection. Even if there are no visible sores, contact with an infected person can cause transmission of genital herpes.

Symptoms can show up one to 30 days or later after having sex. Most people have no symptoms or mild ones.

Women and men with symptoms may notice the following:

- Flu-like feelings (fever, body aches, or swollen glands).
- Small, painful blisters on the genitals, rectum or mouth (often mistaken as a painful pimple or ingrown hair).
- Itching or burning before blisters appear.
- The blister may go away, but you still have herpes; blisters can come back.

Remember: This is a viral infection that can be spread very easily. Even if a person is a virgin, they may contract genital herpes if they come in contact with infected genitals. Unfortunately, condoms do not protect against genital herpes because it is spread through skin-to-skin contact. There is no cure for herpes, but medications can be used to stop or manage outbreaks. You can request a HSV-1 and HSV-2 blood test to confirm if this virus is present.

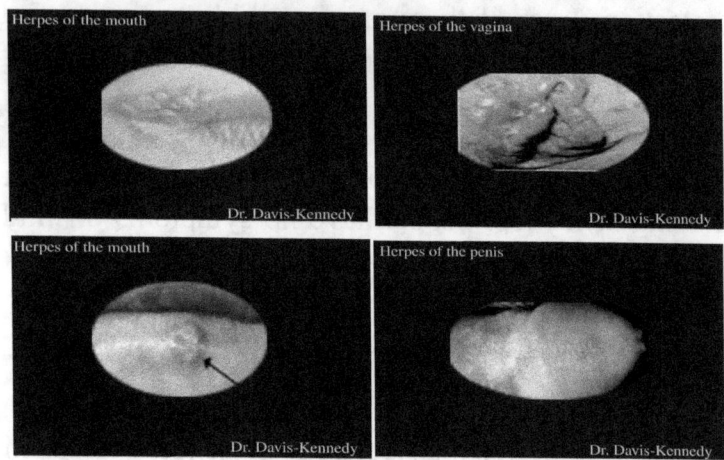

HIV/AIDS

The Human Immunodeficiency Virus (HIV) is the immune system attacker that can lead to development of Acquired Immunodeficiency Syndrome (AIDS). Unlike other infections, the human body cannot get rid of HIV/AIDS. Unfortunately, once you have HIV you have it forever. There is only one way to know if you are infected; you must test by blood or oral fluid analysis.

HIV is often considered the most serious and dangerous STD. This is a virus that you cannot see and symptoms aren't always reliable. Many people who are infected with HIV may not have any symptoms for 10 years or more.

It can be transmitted through vaginal, anal or oral sex with someone, heterosexual or homosexual, that is infected. HIV can also be spread through infected blood, sharing of needles, syringes, or other drug-injection equipment.

Other ways HIV can be contracted:

- Sharing razors or toothbrushes with an infected person.
- Through breast milk and direct contact with the blood or open sores of an infected person.
- Through childbirth (spread from an infected mother to her baby during birth)*

*Medications are commonly used to stop the transmission to the baby.

HIV is a sexually transmitted disease that can be dormant and have an incubation period for an extended amount of time. This means that it can go undetected, even if a person is, in fact, infected.

HIV/AIDS Indicators:

- Flu-like symptoms (the worst flu ever, usually two to four weeks after exposure).
- Fever

- Enlarged lymph nodes
- Unexplained weight loss and/or fatigue
- Diarrhea
- White spots in mouth
- Yeast infection in women that doesn't go away
- Sore throat
- Rash

These symptoms can last anywhere from a few days to several weeks. Even if HIV cannot be detected at the time, it is highly infectious and can be spread to others.

Types of Tests to detect HIV/AIDS:

Antibody tests ("Rapid" tests)—Gives a result based on antibodies to HIV, not the virus itself. It can properly start detection two to eight weeks after infection exposure; most people will have enough antibodies to test precisely. Twelve weeks after initial infection, about 97% of people will have enough antibodies to test accurately.

Antigen tests (RNA tests)—Show a result based on the presence of the virus within the body. These tests are more expensive than antibody tests, so they are not offered in as many places. One to three weeks after infection exposure is usually enough time for a proper result using RNA tests.

Remember: There is no cure for HIV, but there are many different treatment options to manage the virus. This is no longer the disease that you have to die from. If you are not treated and do not take care of your body, it will eventually turn into AIDS, which is a lot more severe.

You must get tested before a new partner and after you have changed partners. If you have unprotected sex, it is recommended you get blood tested two weeks, three months, six months, and a year after the unprotected sexual encounter.

Human Papillomavirus (HPV)

HPV is the most common sexually transmitted infection (STI) according to the CDC. Nearly all sexually active men and women get it at some point in their lives. About 79 million Americans are currently infected, and nearly 14 million new people become infected each year.

You can get HPV by having vaginal, anal or oral sex, as well as genital touching (skin-to-skin contact) with someone who has the disease. Symptoms can show up weeks, months, or years after contact with HPV. Many people have no symptoms at all ever in life.

There are many different types of HPV; women and men can get different types. Different types cause different symptoms such as:

Genital Warts - Single or group of bumpy warts on the genitals. Genital Warts can be small or large, raised or flat, or shaped like a cauliflower. They cause itching or burning around the sex organs. The warts may go away, but they can return at any time because the virus stays in the body forever.

Cancer - Cells become cancerous within the cervix, vulva, vagina, penis, anus, and throat.

This virus is not easily avoided; virgins can get HPV/Genital Warts, and condoms do not protect against Genital Warts being that it is spread through skin-to-skin contact.

Although there is no cure for HPV, there is a vaccine called Gardasil that is safe and effective. The Gardasil vaccine is approved for both males and females between ages nine to 26, and is recommended before the first time having sexual activity or intercourse. This vaccine protects from genital warts and high-risk cancer-causing HPV strands.

Remember: There is no blood test at this time to check for HPV. It cannot be detected in men, but women can request a pap smear to check for HPV. Pap smears are recommended for women between the ages of 21 and 65 years old and can prevent the progression of cervical cancer.

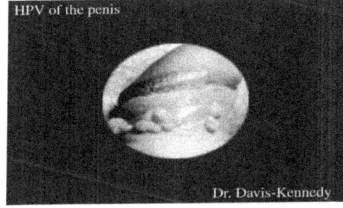
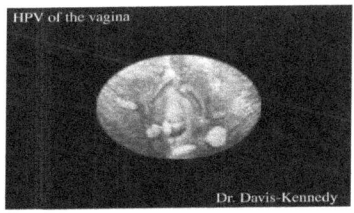
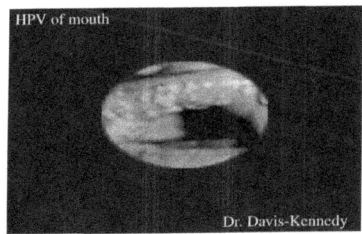

Chapter 6: Other STDs

A lot of the STDs mentioned in previous chapters are amongst the most common of them all. Believe it or not, there are even more sexually transmitted diseases. There is not a lot of mention of Parasitic STDs, but they do exist. It is important that when educating someone on a topic, you give him or her the full scope. So, next we are going to discuss lesser-known STDs, some parasitic, and more bacterial and viral infections as well.

Trichomoniasis (Trich)

Trichomoniasis is a sexually transmitted disease that is caused by infection of a protozoan parasite called Trichomonas Vaginalis. It is considered to be the most common curable STD. In the United States, an estimated 3.7 million people have the infection, but only about 30% develop any symptoms of Trichomoniasis, according to the CDC.

Although symptoms vary, most people who have the parasite cannot tell they are infected at all. It is transferred during vaginal sex. In women, the most commonly infected part of the body is the lower genital tract:

In women: vulva, vagina, or urethra.

In men: inside of the penis (urethra).

If symptoms ever show up, it's usually five to 28 days after having sex with an infected person.

Men with symptoms may have:

- A burning sensation or pain when urinating.
- A watery white drip from penis.
- Frequent urination.

Women with symptoms may have:

- Itching, burning, or irritation in the vagina.
- Fishy or musky odor from the vagina.
- Yellow, greenish, or gray vaginal discharge.
- Vaginal bleeding between periods.

Remember: Trich can be cured with antibiotics. The diagnosis comes from a genital culture in both men and women. Trich is also seen in homosexual women and those who share sex toys without first cleaning them properly.

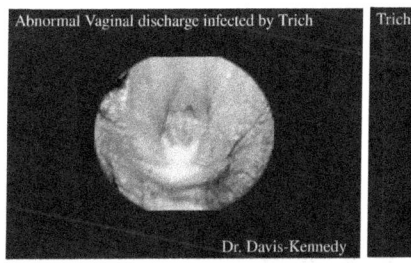
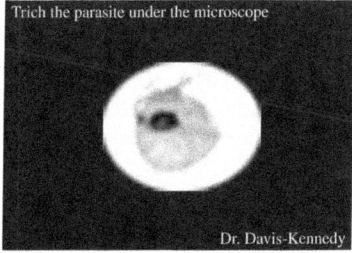
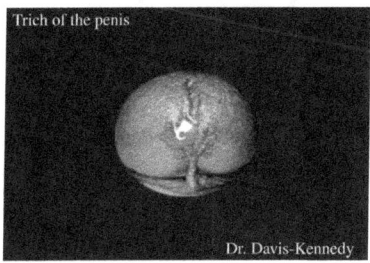

Chancroid

Chancroid is a sexually transmitted genital ulcer disease caused by the bacterium Haemophilus Ducreyi. Although not as common in the United States, it is a relatively common disease in the developing world. Chancroid is transmitted through vaginal and anal sex. Symptoms usually show up one week after having sex.

Symptoms may include:

- One or more painful genital ulcers.
- Lymph node enlargement where the Chancroid is located.

Remember: A genital culture is used to detect Chancroid, and it can be cured with antibiotics. It's common in some regions of Africa and in the Caribbean.

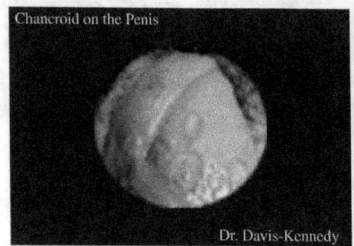

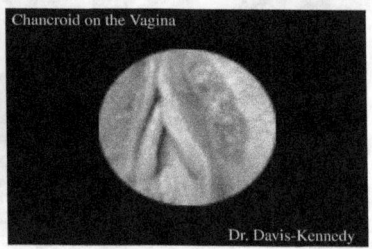

Lymphogranuloma Venereum (LGV)

LGV is a sexually transmitted disease or infection involving the lymph glands in the genital area. It is caused by a specific strain of chlamydia, which comes from bacteria. Lymphogranuloma Venereum is transmitted via vaginal and anal sex.

The occurrence of LGV is highest among sexually active people in tropical or subtropical environments. It has also occurred in some areas of the southern United States.

Symptoms show up three to 30 days after having sex with an infected person.

Symptoms may include:

- Painless small sore on the penis or vagina.

- Enlarged genital lymph nodes.
- Infection can spread to the lymph node in the groin area if not treated.

Remember: A genital culture and blood test is used to detect this disease, and antibiotics cure it. LGV is common in tropical or subtropical climates.

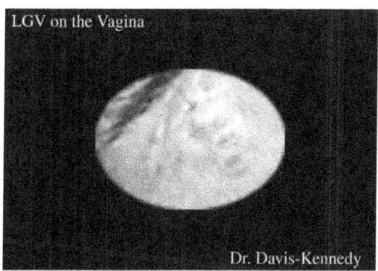
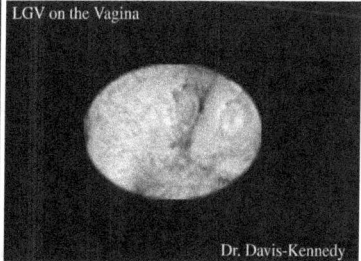

Pediculosis Pubis

Pediculosis Pubis, also known as *Pubic Lice* or *Crabs*, are small parasitic bugs that reside in the pubic area. Pubic lice are parasitic insects found primarily in the pubic or genital area of humans and feed off blood. Pubic lice infestation is found worldwide and occurs in all races, ethnic groups, and levels of society.

Pubic lice are transmitted through bed sheets, sexual contact, vaginal and anal sex, and genital rubbing.

Symptoms show up immediately or up to one day after being infected.

Symptoms may include:

- Itching in the genital area.
- Visible nits (lice/bug eggs).
- Visible crawling lice/bugs.

Remember: Pubic Lice/Crabs can be cured with anti-parasitic medication. It is less commonly found in eyebrows, eyelashes, beard, mustache, armpit, perianal area, groin, trunk, and scalp. A healthcare provider seeing the bugs with or without a microscope detects this parasitic disease.

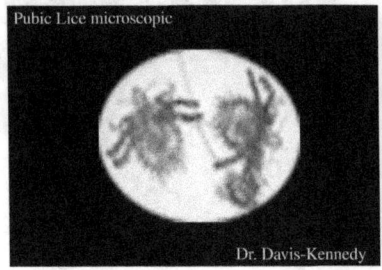
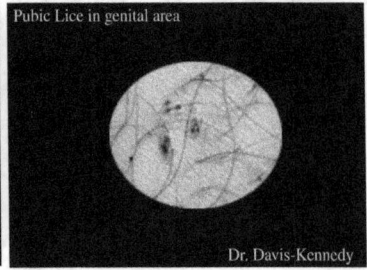

Scabies

Human *scabies* is caused by an infestation of the skin by the human itch mite (Sarcoptes scabiei var. hominis). These very small parasitic bugs burrow into the upper layer of the skin where it lives and lays its eggs.

Scabies are spread by direct, prolonged, skin-to-skin

contact with a person who is infected. Sexual activities are a great way to become inhabited by these mites.

For first time scabies, symptoms may take as long as four to six weeks to show up. It is imperative to remember that an infected person can spread scabies at all times, even if symptoms are not present. In a person who has had scabies before, symptoms usually appear much sooner, usually one to four days after re-exposure.

Symptoms may include:

- Intense itching in these areas: the wrist, elbow, armpit, between fingers, nipple, penis, waist, belt-line, and buttocks.
- Pimple-like skin rash.

Remember: The healthcare provider seeing the bugs, with or without a microscope, detects this parasitic disease. If detected, Scabies can be cured with anti-parasitic medication.

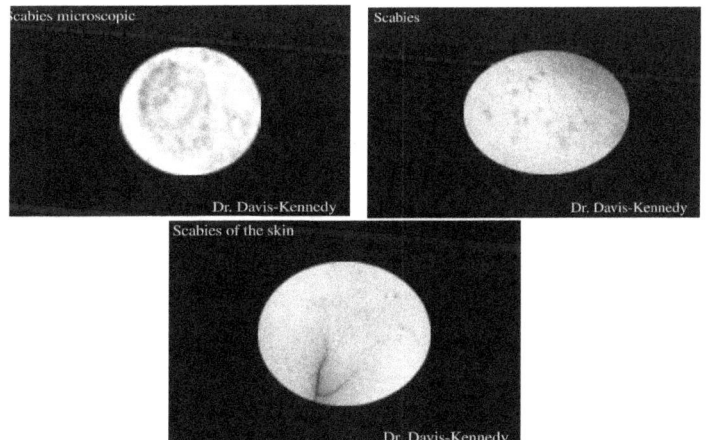

Molluscum

Molluscum Contagiosum is an infection caused by a poxvirus. The visual effect is usually a benign, mild skin disease characterized by lesions or growths on the body. Molluscum may occur anywhere on the body; i.e. the face, neck, arms, legs, abdomen, and genital area, all at once or region based. The lesions are rarely found on the palms of the hands or the soles of the feet, so if you notice lesions in these areas, it may be something else.

Molluscum usually spreads by direct skin-to-skin contact with an infected person. This can be transmitted when having sexual intercourse with a person who is infected, thus making it a sexually transmitted disease.

Symptoms can appear two to 12 weeks after exposure; however, it can take years for it to appear to the eye.

Symptoms may include:

- Lesion/bump that is small, raised, and usually white, pink, or flesh-colored with a dimple or pit in the center.
- Pearly-appearing bump that is smooth and firm.
- Bumps/lesions that may be itchy, sore, red, and/ or swollen.

Remember: This disease is detected by inspection by your healthcare provider. There are medications available that you can take orally or apply directly to the skin. However, your healthcare provider may burn or freeze the bumps away. Within six to 12 months, Molluscum Contagiosum typically resolves without scarring but can take as long as four years to do so. Since the virus lives only on the top layer of skin, once the lesions are gone the virus is gone and you cannot spread it to others.

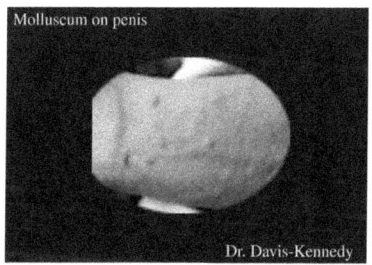
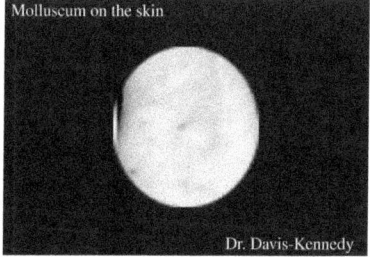

Chapter 7: Student

Do's and Don'ts

As a student, it may be difficult to discuss sex with your parents, especially if they are not open to hearing your concerns and questions. However, the reality is that you will have sex one day! Hopefully, later than sooner, but whenever that time comes, you must make sure you are properly prepared. Don't just settle with the rumors amongst your friends, or the things you've seen on TV; actually take the step to get educated about all things sex.

Before you actually have "The Talk," you may want to consider a few things. Ideally, you want to have a comfortable, inviting and calm environment so that your parents know you are serious about discussing sex. It's important to have an open discussion about it, no matter how embarrassing or scary it may be. Having this conversation could mean life or death if you go out in the world without being properly equipped with information.

Here is some recommended advice for "The Talk":

- It is important that you ask questions to root out

any misinformation. Study all the information in chapters 1 – 5 to make sure you know the changes your body will go through and know the names of the STDs, how to contract them and the symptoms for each.

- Be open-minded and patient. This may or may not be the first time your parent has had the sex talk, especially if you have siblings. So, be open with them and don't get upset if they become angry. This will make way for open and honest dialogue.

- Talk with your parent, not at your parent. Many parents go into lecture mode when having discussions. Remember, the idea is to keep it a conversation so that he or she will feel comfortable enough to ask questions and be as a parent.

- If by chance you have had sexual intercourse or some sort of sexual activity, do not feel scared or approach your parent in a negative manner. This will cause them not to talk to you again about sexual issues. Remember, you must be comfortable, but so should they. Just take a deep breath and be understanding so you both can move forward.

- Be sympathetic. Remember your parent has to hear about your interest in possibly having sex soon. This is something they probably haven't even imaged yet, so they may be in shock initially, or have mixed emotions.

- It's very important for you to continuously promote being approachable. Stay open with your parents. Don't hide things from them. This will make room for future conversations, which could prevent unwanted pregnancies, STDs or premature sexual encounters.

- It is important that you use your family values discussed with your parents in your decision-making. Telling them your feelings about sex would probably help them trust you more.

- If you are already sexually active, or plan to become active soon, schedule a doctor's appointment to go over contraceptives and health screenings. It's a good idea to do this with your parents because they can help you make a decision on which contraceptive to use. They also are aware of information that you don't know about yourself just yet.

Chapter 8: Advice for the Student

Sex is a risky activity. It shouldn't be looked at as just fun or something that people just do.

Below are some things to remember before engaging in any sexual activity:

- Talk to your parent. This is and always will be the first thing to do before engaging in sex. Your parents will give you more information than you would know and they could help you consider things you wouldn't have otherwise thought to remember.

- A doctor can provide you with contraceptives, even more health and sexual knowledge, and also make you aware of your health status.

- For the girls, you should start birth control before you have sex in order to prevent pregnancy.

- Make sure you understand the genitalia, what STDs are and what they can do to your body.

- Get tested for STDs before you decide to have sex; be sure your partner has been tested as well and that they make you aware of their sexual history. Being sexually responsible means asking tough questions, so always ask if the person you're about to have sex with has ever been tested and have ever had an STD before.

- Get to know your future sexual partner very well, and enter a monogamous relationship. This means you both will only be having sex with one another.

- Examine your partner's genital area thoroughly before sexual activity. If you see any bumps, sores, irritated areas or anything that looks out of the ordinary, do not go on to have sex with them. You should question them about it, then advise them to go see a doctor.

- Learn how to use both male and female condoms and other contraceptives.

- If you plan to engage in oral sex, make sure you purchase a Dental Dam in advance and only have oral sex when it is present. No exceptions!

- Don't ask your friends about sex; more often than not, they will offer wrong information or myths.

- *ABSOLUTELY* do not have unprotected sex. Any time you engage in sex, even oral sex, always protect yourself. It doesn't matter how much you trust a person, or how great they look. STDs are passed on through unprotected sex, so protect yourself and use contraceptives. Note: birth control does not protect you from

STDs, it only protects from getting pregnant. So always use birth control and other forms of contraceptives.

- Do not have sex with people you do not know well.

Chapter 9: Wrap Up

How can you prevent yourself from getting STDs?

It is vital to remember to always protect yourself from sexually transmitted diseases (STDs). You can do this with condoms or by abstaining from sex. Unfortunately, condoms do not always prevent you from getting an STD. There are some sexually transmitted infections that can be passed from the areas that condoms don't cover. All in all, abstinence is the best way not to get an STD. But the reality is people will have sex. So, if you do, wrap it up and wear a condom every time.

As you have read, there are many STDs that are bacterial, viral, and parasitic. If you get a bacteria or parasitic STD, you have been given a second chance because there is a cure for these. If you catch a viral STD, this cannot be cured, unfortunately. Once you got it, you own it! However there are treatments, so it's not looked at as a death sentence, but you can die from some viral infections.

Sexually transmitted diseases are transmitted via skin-to-skin contact and through vaginal, oral, and anal sex. Keep in mind, virgins can get STDs too. As crazy as it sounds, it's true. If a person that is still a virgin engages in sexual activities like touching genitals with another person that has a sexually transmitted disease, then they too can be exposed to it and then have an

STD.

Remember, it should always be your top priority to use male or female condoms properly every time you have sex. If you have a latex allergy, no worries!! There are condoms made out of polyurethane that can be used, such as Trojan Supra or Durex Avanti.

For oral sex, be sure to use a Dental Dam. Being in a long-term mutually-monogamous relationship with a partner who has been tested and has negative STD test results will decrease your risks of getting a STD, but you still must use protection no matter what.

When a person engages in risky sexual activities, there are usually always consequences. Don't be the person trying to figure out how to fix the problem, when you can be the person preventing the problem from happening. Remember to make responsible decisions, and be knowledgeable about sex.

Glossary

Anal Sex—The insertion and thrusting of an erect penis into an anus for sexual pleasure.

Anti-parasitic Medications—Medications that are indicated for the treatment of parasitic diseases.

Anti-viral Medications—Medications that are indicated for the treatment of viral diseases.

Antibiotics—A type of antimicrobial used in the treatment and prevention of bacterial infections. They may either kill or inhibit the growth of bacteria.

Antibody/Antigen Test—Tests done to find certain antibodies that attack red blood cells.

Asymptomatic—Producing or showing no symptoms.

Bacterial Infection—An infection caused by bacteria.

Bacterium—A microscopic living organism, usually one-celled, that can be found everywhere.

Bodily Fluids—Liquids originating from inside the bodies of living humans.

Cancer—The disease caused by an uncontrolled division of abnormal cells in a part of the body.

Chancroid—A venereal infection causing ulceration of the lymph nodes in the groin.

Chlamydia—A common sexually transmitted infection caused by a very small bacterium.

Contraceptives—A device or drug used in order to prevent pregnancy.

Crabs—(Slang for Pubic Lice) Parasitic insects that can infest in the genital area.

Dental Dam—A thin sheet of latex used as a prophylactic device during oral sex.

Diagnosis—The identification of the nature of an illness or other problem by examination of the symptoms.

Discharge—A secretion coming from the vagina or penis.

Fungal Infection—An infection caused by fungus.

Genital Culture—A swab analysis of the genitals for the identification of pathogen, whether bacterial, viral, or fungal.

Genital Warts—A small growth occurring in the anal or genital areas caused by Human Papillomavirus (HPV). It is spread by sexual contact.

Genitals—External reproductive organs.

Gonorrhea—A sexually transmitted disease involving inflammatory discharge from the urethra or vagina.

Haemophilus Ducreyi—A fastidious gram-negative coccobacillus causing the sexually transmitted disease chancroid.

Hepatitis B—A severe form of viral hepatitis transmitted in infected blood, causing fever, debility, and jaundice.

Hepatitis C—Inflammation of the liver caused by a severe form of viral hepatitis transmitted through infected blood.

Herpes—A virus causing contagious sores, most often around the mouth or on the genitals.

Heterosexual—Sexually attracted to people of the opposite sex.

HIV/AIDS—Human Immunodeficiency Virus (HIV) is a virus that attacks the immune system, the body's natural defense system. This causes Acquired

Immunodeficiency Syndrome (AIDS), a chronic, potentially life-threatening condition.

Homosexual—Sexually attracted to people of one's own sex.

HPV—Human papilloma virus, a virus with subtypes that cause diseases in humans ranging from common warts to cervical cancer.

HSV 1 and HSV2 Blood Test—Testing performed to identify an acute herpes infection or to detect herpes antibodies.

Infertility—The inability to achieve pregnancy.

Inflammation—A localized physical condition in which part of the body becomes reddened, swollen, hot, and often painful, especially as a reaction to injury or infection.

Intercourse—The act of having sex.

Lymphogranuloma Venereum—A contagious venereal disease caused by various strains of chlamydia.

Molluscum Contagiosum—A chronic viral disorder of the skin characterized by groups of small, smooth, painless pinkish nodules.

Neisseria Gonorrhea—Type of diplococci bacteria responsible for the sexually transmitted infection gonorrhea.

Oral Sex—The insertion and thrusting of an erect penis or vagina into the mouth for sexual pleasure.

Pap Smear—A procedure to test for cervical cancer in women.

Parasitic Infection—An infectious disease caused or transmitted by a parasite.

Pediculosis Pubis ("Crabs" or "Pubic Lice")—A disease caused by the pubic lice, Pthirus pubis, a parasitic insect that infest human pubic hair.

Protozoan Parasite—A one-celled organism (called protists) that live as a parasite.

Pubic Lice—Slang for crabs, parasitic insects that can infest in the genital area.

Reproductive Tract—A part of the reproductive system.

Sarcoptes Scabiei Var. Hominis—Little mites that cause scabies by burrowing into the upper layer of the skin to live and lay its eggs.

Scabies—A contagious skin disease marked by

itching and small raised red spots, caused by the itch mite (Sarcoptes Scabiei Var. Hominis).

Sexual Activities—Associated with sexual intercourse, but not only the act itself.

Sexually Transmitted Disease (STD)—Any of various diseases or infections that are usually transmitted by direct sexual contact and that include some that may be contracted by other than sexual means.

Sexually Transmitted Infections (STI)—Any of various diseases or infections that are usually transmitted by direct sexual contact and that include some that may be contracted by other than sexual means.

Skin-to-skin contact—Touching another person's skin with any part of your skin.

Trichomonas Vaginalis—An anaerobic flagellated protozoan parasite and the causative agent of **trichomoniasis**.

Trichomoniasis—An infection caused by parasitic trichomonads, chiefly affecting the urinary tract, vagina, or digestive system.

Unprotected Sex—An act of sexual intercourse performed without the use of a condom.

Urethra—The duct by which urine is conveyed out of the body from the bladder.

Vaginal Sex—The insertion and thrusting of an erect penis into a vagina for sexual pleasure.

Venereal Disease (VD)—A disease typically contracted by sexual contact with a person already infected; a sexually transmitted disease.

Viral Infection—A disease that can be caused by different kinds of viruses.

Viruses—An infective agent that typically consists of a nucleic acid molecule in a protein coat, is too small to be seen by light microscopy, and is able to multiply only within the living cells of a host.

References

Center for Disease Control. (2014). Chlamydia CDC fact sheet. Retrieved from http://www.cdc.gov/std/chlamydia/stdfact-chlamydia.htm

Center for Disease Control. (2014). Gonorrhea CDC fact sheet. Retrieved from http://www.cdc.gov/std/chlamydia/stdfact-gonorrhea.htm

Center for Disease Control. (2014). Hepatitis B FAQs for the public. Retrieved from http://www.cdc.gov/hepatitis/hbv/bfaq.htm

Center for Disease Control. (2014). Hepatitis C FAQs for the public. Retrieved from http://www.cdc.gov/hepatitis/hcv/cfaq.htm

Center for Disease Control. (2014). Genital Herpes CDC fact sheet. Retrieved from http://www.cdc.gov/std/herpes/stdfact-herpes.htm

Center for Disease Control. (2015). Genital HPV infection fact sheet. Retrieved from http://www.cdc.gov/std/hpv/stdfact-hpv.htm

Center for Disease Control. (2015). Trichomonas CDC fact sheet. Retrieved from http://www.cdc.gov/std/trichomonas/stdfact-trichomoniasis.htm

Center for Disease Control. (2015). Chancroid. Retrieved

from http://www.cdc.gov/std/tg2015/chancroid.htm

Center for Disease Control. (2015). Lymphogranuloma Venereum. Retrieved from http://www.cdc.gov/std/tg2015/lgv.htm

Center for Disease Control. (2014). Pubic Lice. Retrieved from http://www.cdc.gov/parasites/lice/pubic/

Center for Disease Control. (2014). Scabies. Retrieved from http://www.cdc.gov/parasites/scabies/

Center for Disease Control. (2015). Molluscum Contagiosum. Retrieved from http://www.cdc.gov/poxvirus/molluscum-contagiosum/

Center for Disease Control. (2014). Syphilis CDC fact sheet. Retrieved from http://www.cdc.gov/std/syphilis/stdfact-syphilis.htm

Center for Disease Control. (2015). About HIV/AIDS. Retrieved from http://www.cdc.gov/hiv/basics/whatIshiv.html

"Consumer Assets." *Wed MD*, 2011, img.webmd.com/dtmcms/live/webmd/consumer_assets/site_images/media/medical/hw/h9991308-001.jpg.

"Growth and Your 13- to 18-Year-Old." Edited by Mary L. Gavin, *KidsHealth*, The Nemours Foundation, Jan. 2015, kidshealth.org/en/parents/growth-13-to-18.html.

"Male Genitals ." *Amazon News*, 2012, s3.amazonaws.com/classconnection/742/flashcards/7831742/png/male_genital_structures-14C721531C33C92943A.png.

"Menstruation and the Menstrual Cycle." *Womenshealth. gov*, 6 Feb. 2017, www.womenshealth.gov/a-z-topics/menstruation-and-menstrual-cycle.

"Ovulation Causes ." *Medindia*, 2002, www.medindia.net/patients/patientinfo/images/ovulation-causes.jpg+.

San Franscisco AIDS Foundation. (2015). HIV test window periods. Retrieved from http://www.sfaf.org/hiv-info/testing/hiv-test-window-periods.html

www.ingramcontent.com/pod-product-compliance
Lightning Source LLC
Chambersburg PA
CBHW071538080526
44588CB00011B/1719